WARNING: MAY CAUSE YOU TO

LAUNCH YOUR HR CAREER

NATALIE ELLIS

LAUNCH YOUR HR CAREER

All the best wishes
for your career!
Natalie x

NATALIE ELLIS

natalieellishr.com

Layout Design: Amy Bradley

www.amybradley.co.uk

Published by Rebox HR Ltd
ISBN 978-1-5272-7139-5

"TO MY FAMILY, THANK YOU FOR MAKING MY DREAMS REALITY,
ALWAYS SAYING WHAT I CAN DO, NOT WHAT I CAN'T DO.

FOR MY FRIENDS; THIS WOULDN'T HAVE HAPPENED WITHOUT YOUR SUPPORT, FRIENDSHIP NEVER ENDS"

LAUNCH YOUR HR CAREER

NATALIE ELLIS

CONTENTS LIST:

FOREWORD BY SHAKIL BUTT

How does one 'get into' HR? You would think that would be an easy straight forward question to answer. There are a number of routes into the profession whether choosing HR as a career path, deliberately transitioning from another industry or accidentally 'falling' into HR. This book is an invaluable aid to anyone who has opted to become a people professional. Natalie Ellis is the perfect person to share her insights into the 'ups and downs' of 'getting into' HR and has very real 'warts and all' approach.

With over 10 years of experience going from in house support and lead on HR to providing services as a HR consultant, there is not much that Natalie has not experienced. Having recently completed her CIPD qualification means that Natalie has given blood, sweat and tears to earn her professional standing in the HR community. She has her own successful award winning HR blog, is an active CIPD branch member and has even launched the hashtag #HRActofKindness engaging with the wider global HR profession. Natalie has grown her visibility and influence over a short space of time and consequently is an in demand speaker at HR conferences and events so it is no exaggeration to say that Natalie is a HR professional that understands her own industry.

This is not yet another business book with 'a how to' approach guide because there is simply not one size fits all. Rather it is an adventure and the symbol of the rocket is very apt, so prepare to get ready to launch your career as a HR professional.

Rightly so, Natalie's starting point is around purpose – not the organisational purpose but your own and she underscores how critical it is that you find your own purpose in the world, for without it, it is impossible to then effect the direction of not just your career but your life as well.

If purpose is the starting point, Natalie suggests that the next ingredient to have a successful career is a mixture of ambition and motivation, to feel the fear and do it anyway. To be brave and knock on that door, to make that call, to reach out for support and see what happens. This can-do attitude is essential because it is liberating. Natalie emphasises the importance of self-belief because she knows all too well the mountains that need traversing are not easy and the temptation to give up is far too great at times but the peaks are brought closer with every single step made easier with the right foundation. She calls it as it is.

There are no substitutes for rolling up your sleeves and getting 'stuck in' and finding your boundaries and pushing past them to learn that the only limits on what you can do are the ones that you impose on yourself. This growth mindset is not necessarily new, but Natalie shares the importance of accepting that there will knock backs and failures but they themselves do not define you rather how you respond to them does. This resilience building is the secret weapon of the HR professional as Natalie stresses that it will definitely not be 'sunshine and rainbows' and there are many dark sides and soul-destroying work practices to fix before you can really effect change in your organisation.

The timing of this book is perfect with seeing what HR is capable of and HR professionals starting to realise their value in the world of work. This book will be a great assist to the adventure that lies ahead. If you are looking for support and inspiration to help you get to your end point then relax in the knowledge, Natalie has written this book with you in mind to do exactly what it says on the tin. Now go and be brilliant and make your mark in the ever changing world of work.

INTRODUCTION

I am often asked how I became a Human Resources Consultant, and Director of Rebox HR Ltd, when my first job was in a travel agency. It isn't too long a story. Why not grab a coffee, and let me tell you what happened?

When I was five years old I thought I knew what I wanted to do when I grew up. One of my friends said he would like to be a Policeman. Another intended to be a vet, a nurse, and so on. I told my teacher that I was going to work for British Airways as a stewardess at Heathrow Airport. I loved the shiny buttons on their uniforms and the pride they had as they served customers with a beaming smile.

I realise now that all I wanted was for Mum and Dad to be proud of me. I didn't become a member of British Airways' cabin crew, instead my sister got a job working for BA, and Mum and Dad are proud of my success in the HR profession. Whilst I will always be grateful to them for doing everything they could, to help me.

Life doesn't always go according to plan, but the job that is right for you is waiting to happen. Don't lose sight of it, or your passion. Whether you are choosing a University, or course which could lead to it. Stepping into the employment arena for the first time or acquiring the skills to move forward later on. Carry on persevering as I did until you find it and can make it your own. I wish you all the luck in the world. I hope that this book will help and inspire you, to get onto the career ladder, consider a career change or even take the next step in your journey.

With love, and best wishes,

Natalie x

PART I: GETTING STARTED

Look
for the
RAINBOW
in every
storm

CHAPTER 1: Following My Passion

1. My first Job

I had my first job interview when I was eighteen years old. I was about to finish my A level examinations in Business, Travel and Tourism. I wanted to work for Lunn Poly travel agency in Maidenhead, later known as Thomson Holidays, and I wasn't going to wait for my results. I was eager, and excited about getting my first job. So the day after I finished school I found myself sending clients all over the world on the holiday of their dreams, but faery tales are a funny thing. They don't always last, and two years later my business brain had kicked in. Although I enjoyed the job, I felt restless. I needed more. I wanted to learn how a business worked. The ways in which an employee might influence this, but I didn't know how I would go about it. Other than that I needed more experience, and would have to work for another company to get it.

2. Changing jobs to develop my skills

It wasn't long before I was taken on by an American company, as an Administrator in their busy sales team. I was quickly moved into project management to support one of their major clients, BT. It was exactly what I needed. I was able to hone my customer service skills in this role. I discovered the importance of problem solving, and it also became an opportunity to develop my existing administrative skills. All of which serve me well to this day. I stayed in this job for a long time until I knew I had to move on, if I was going to develop my business career. One day when I was at lunch with a colleague, she suggested that I would be the perfect candidate for a job in HR. The more I thought about this I realised that it might well be possible to make a difference to an organisation, by supporting the people who worked within it.

3. My Career in HR was about to begin

I made the decision to move into a new industry, and it was a struggle initially to identify where I would fit into the workplace. What was my desired role? I wasn't sure. I didn't know enough about the options which would be available to me, and I soon learned that HR was a highly competitive field. If I wanted a job I would more than likely have to send in a lot of applications. Then attend at least several interviews before receiving an offer of employment, if I was fortunate, but knowing what would be involved made it easier for me to accept the process. Instead of being daunted by what was happening, or allowing it to damage my confidence, I persevered.

4. The important questions I asked myself

I asked myself three questions which I hope will also help you now, to make the right decision about your career path. Don't worry if you don't know the answers straight away. I didn't, and that doesn't matter. All you need to do is try to be as specific as you can with your replies, and go back to them from time to time. The questions are as follows:

a. Why did I want to work in HR?

It was important to know exactly what had attracted me to being an HR professional. Some people are drawn to a specific industry, or family run business which they know something about. At that time my answer was based more on the skills and personality traits I would be bringing to the job. I enjoyed a challenge, and I was determined to succeed. So I hoped to stand out from the crowd, by being passionate about my future in HR.

b. What exactly did I want to do as an HR professional?

This was a little more difficult to work out because of my lack of knowledge. I wasn't even sure how far up the career ladder I could go. My secret wish was to reach the stars! It soon became apparent that if this had any chance of becoming a reality I would have to learn as much as I could about industry and business, to find out which areas interested me the most. I would also need to consider getting qualifications. I realised later that having learned a lot about business had become one of my strengths. When I was working alongside managers who had been doing the job for years.

c. How would I get my desired role?

Most career paths make detours, and having considered this possibility beforehand, I could look at my job search in a different way. I became adaptable when thinking about building the Curriculum Vitae I would need for the career I had set my heart on. I decided that if the role I wanted wasn't available, I would look for an alternate position which might still get me there. Employers place great importance on qualifications. Suffice to say here that I didn't need any qualifications, other than my examination results, to take my first step into HR as an Administrator. If I wanted to be promoted later to an advisory role I would need a CIPD Level 3 Certificate in HR Practice, and I started to shift my mindset in preparation for the studying I would have to do.

5. Being inspired by the Stars

How was I able to think like this? Believe it or not, my early drive and motivation originated in 1996, when the Spice Girls shot to the top of the charts. Their fantastic success excited, and inspired me. You may now be following your favourite celebrity's progress. There is usually something to be learned from his or her success, but all I knew then was that I loved the Spice Girls' music. I also wanted everything in Emma Bunton's wardrobe! It was a long time ago, but there is one thing that has stayed with me. All the hard work they put in, to become what seemed at the time, an overnight success.

They sacrificed further education, employment opportunities, and lived on state benefits for two years to become the most successful girl group of the nineties. Can you imagine Victoria Beckham collecting her dole money in Maidenhead town centre? No! Neither can I, but the Spice Girls were following their passion to make their dream come true. I also wanted to be the best that I could be, but as an HR professional. I kept this thought at the forefront of my mind when applying for jobs, and later, as I was going to work.

6. Going for Interviews

Once I began attending interviews, the enthusiasm to succeed and desire to learn had to replace my obvious lack of experience. I was effectively a strong administrator, with customer service experience, applying for a role in HR. These were the qualities my first HR employer noticed, during my ninth interview. I was offered an Administrator's position at the end of our conversation.

It would have been easy to feel disheartened by such a long process, but don't forget. I was channeling my inner Ginger Spice. The Group had sacked their first manager before Geri Halliwell's determination to work with a successful songwriter, Elliot Kennedy, proved to be a turning point in their career. He went on to produce their second hit record, despite being reluctant initially to work with them. Geri's passion to make the group a success persuaded him to change his mind. The Spice Girls were confident and unique, but it does take a lot of confidence to stand out from the crowd. Especially if you want to create a successful career, in HR.

Always follow your dreams. Never give up.

"Swing it. Shake it,"

and show them just how good you are!

CHAPTER 2: Knowledge Is Power

I believe that there is a star in all of us, and I was by this time desperate to become mine! The problem was I was missing one of my super powers... Knowledge. Nevertheless I carried on being my own cheerleader. I persevered because I still wanted to have the job of my dreams. I had a lot to learn but, with the experience I would be gaining along the way, I also didn't stop believing in my success.

1. I kept a positive mindset

I looked for as many positives as I could in my job search, and I thought about transferable skills. Much to my surprise I found that I had a lot, despite not having had an HR background. I started out in customer services, but HR could be thought of in terms of an internal customer service department. So I played to this strength. If I had been from a financial background, HR analytics might well have been the perfect fit, and there were many possibilities the more I thought about it.

I had also quietly started to build business relationships through networking, and social media. I talked to the few professionals I knew, to gain their insight into my employment situation. The jobs I applied for at the start of my career came from advertisements, but I would highly recommend that you also think about the possibility of becoming a passive candidate. Some employers prefer to obtain their staff by word of mouth, instead of a job board.

2. Online recruitment

There were plenty of agencies to approach which had HR divisions, and this made it easier to find entry level roles.

Specialist agencies too, like Ashley Kate HR, but I looked at the ones which were prominent in my area. Employers were also recruiting directly from job boards like Indeed, Reed, or Total Jobs. This is what I found when using online recruitment in my search:

a. I could look for job openings at any time of the day or night, and be contacted by email. Some online recruiters were prepared to set up interviews, as a video call. I liked doing this, but appreciate that it probably wasn't for everyone back then. Although talking to each other online has now become an everyday occurrence.
b. I had to accept that there would be an increase in the number of applications for the jobs I was interested in, if they were posted online. They were more readily available, and recruiters could easily reach outside the area I wanted to work in. This would have been useful if I was looking to relocate. Or lived in a small town or village where there weren't a lot of the jobs I was looking for.
c. Some careers sites were badly designed, making their application processes more difficult to use. This could have been frustrating, and stressful.
d. I might have been invited to attend a pre-screening interview online. Recruiters often use these now to reduce the number of candidates for a job. The application process would have been less personal, than speaking by telephone or face to face.
e. In some cases the job description and employee specification hadn't been well drafted, leaving me with a lot of questions. I didn't want to apply for a job that might not be suitable for me, but instead of being able to pick up the phone to

discuss it further, email contact was preferred by the recruiter.

f. I didn't know if my CV would match the recruiters' online keyword search. This tool wouldn't necessarily be used by a small company or business who were advertising locally offline, or had I been discovered by word of mouth.

3. Similarities between HR and Marketing jobs

Although I wasn't tempted to join a marketing team, I did think about the similarities to the skills I would need to work in HR. I didn't find out the answer to my questions until later. Both professions are connected in a lot of ways, and can work collaboratively to increase their employers' brand awareness. When a business is running smoothly, this isn't just because the processes are operating like clockwork. It is more often than not due to the relationship between the departments. All of which should be aligned to the same goal. This sounds like a basic concept, but fails on many occasions to be put into place.

It begins with recruitment which can receive significant support from a marketing department. The team can provide giveaways to attract candidates; design brochures, or a promotional campaign on social media. On one occasion I undertook a project, to design and implement the careers page on the company website. This included recruitment advertisements; corporate social responsibility processes, and communications to employees via a company newsletter. Again this was managed, and produced, in collaboration with the marketing team.

I soon realised that it would have been beneficial to share each other's team meetings. Especially in relation to content marketing when there should be consistency in communications. Job descriptions need to be written in a certain way, for example when dealing with graduate recruitment. It's highly competitive, so companies have to hold themselves out for the right reasons. Instead of HR's factual job description which gives the necessary information and is the starting point of the process, a marketing team has the skills to create a catchy advertisement to attract the best candidates.

4. Returning to work as a Parent

This wasn't what I was doing at the start of my HR career, but I did think about it. As part of the mindset change I was going through to become a member of HR. I was curious whether my job search would have been any different if I had been approaching it as a new parent, or following a career break. It would undoubtedly be a daunting experience. I learned more about this later, from people I worked with who had gone through the process. These are some of the things they told me:

a. Putting themselves first in going back to work had made some of them feel guilty, and this shouldn't have been the case. Being back at work can be a fulfilling, exciting, and rewarding experience for a parent.
b. Their priorities had to change. So it was important to be realistic about the expectations they had for their child, and themselves. What was the child's routine? Did they need childcare, or support from another family member?
c. It was helpful to talk to other working parents who had given them advice.
d. They had looked for the job which would be the best for their family, and them. Making sure they would enjoy it.
e. They considered past work achievements, and

experience. Had they learned any other skills relevant to the job during their absence from work?

f. It had been a good idea to update their Linkedin profile, and reach out to their network. They didn't know where those conversations might have led.
g. By being themselves at the interview, their confidence didn't disappear. They tried not to compare themselves to other candidates who had different priorities. Also accepting that they still had a lot to offer prospective employers, and being surprised at how quickly they settled into the swing of things once they were given the job.
h. A lot of them wanted to prove themselves in the workplace as quickly as possible, but that sometimes became frustrating. It was important to remain open minded because it did take time to adjust to being back at work. A lot of patience too. Those who dealt best with the adjustment had planned their return. Making the transition seem less overwhelming than they thought it would be.

5. Looking for promotion as a new role

If you are looking for a promotion in the company or business where you work, the best advice I can give you is to try to excel in all of your existing tasks. Push yourself outside your comfort zone. Look at your strengths, and the areas where you need improvement, then throw yourself into the latter. If an opportunity arises to work on a project or task that is different to what you would normally do, then give it a go! We are often expected to be a Jack or Jill of all trades in the workplace, and by giving the right impression through the quality of our work, this enables us to stand out. It can take a while to be given promotion, if at all. But the extra effort you put into the job you have will also provide you with a solid grounding, if you go on to apply elsewhere for a new position.

I believe that it's never too late to ask for promotion, or begin a new career! Your date of birth is simply a number at the end of the day, and bears no reflection on your capability to do a good job. Life is too short, not to have the career of your dreams. If you have not worked or studied HR in the past, but have transferable skills as I did, then why not apply for an HR Administration role? Making sure you specify on your CV that you would like to study for, or work in HR. Otherwise recruiters might try to steer you back to the career path you were on, last time you worked.

If you want to study HR while gaining experience doing the job, why not think about getting a Level 3 Certificate in HR Practice? Again, as I did. If you don't want to do a full time University course, there are plenty of options available to study for a CIPD qualification whilst you are working. I realised that the best option for me would be distance learning, because I had worked full time since I left the Sixth Form. Some Colleges and Universities also offer part time studying options in the evening.

BE YOUR OWN CHEERLEADER.

Stay motivated!

CHAPTER 3: The Interviews

Many congratulations! All the hard work you put into your job search is now paying off. A date for your interview has finally arrived. I expect you'll be as excited as I was. It's important to celebrate the milestones in life, and this is most definitely one of them. Also to use the time afterwards, to prepare for what will come next. It will give you the best possible chance of getting the job.

When I started writing HR Professional, How To Kickstart Your Career, I decided that it wouldn't be a text book. If it was there would be a longer chapter than this on interviews. I wanted instead to share with you what I remember most about getting started on the career ladder. The frustrations and heartache which other candidates and I went through. How I dealt with having so many interviews before I was given a job, and came out stronger because of it.

1. Preparing for the interview

These are some of the things I did before an interview:

a. I researched my future employer and found out as much as I could, so that I could talk knowledgeably about the organisation I wanted to join.
b. I decided what I was going to wear. I didn't want to be rushing around at the last minute, searching for the right outfit, and it's always important to be well presented. The competition for jobs is high, and the overall impression we give is important. Whether we are applying to a large corporate, or family business.
c. I worked out how I would get to the interview

so that I would have plenty of time on the day, especially if I was using public transport. It would have been fantastic to think of a Knight in shining armour or Superhero suddenly appearing at the last minute, if I was going to be late, but how often does that actually happen? Far better to have sorted out my journey in advance, and be well prepared.

d. I thought about what I was going to say. Deciding on a few points that I could easily remember and wanted to get across at the interview, based on the skills I would be bringing to the job. I was hoping to impress the interviewer. This preparation can help show an interest in the job, social skills, and passion for HR. The focus should always be on what we have to offer. Not on what we don't!

2. At the Interview

a. I always tried to remember to smile, and be professional. Even though I was feeling nervous. That's only natural.
b. The employer was obviously thinking about whether I was the right candidate for the job. If I would fit into an existing team but didn't have the requisite skills, how quickly would I be able to learn them? I was sometimes asked competency based questions, like tell me about the time when... This is an artificial practise which usually seemed irrelevant to the job, but I still tried to think ahead. To be prepared for it, and what else I might be asked.
c. I wasn't afraid to ask questions, to find out as much as possible about what would be expected of me. If the job wasn't quite what I thought it was going to be, then I wanted to

know before I started. Letting myself in for something which wasn't right for me could have led to performance issues later on. Even the inability to pass a probationary period. Asking questions also made the interview seem more human, and gave the employer and myself an opportunity to interact naturally with each other.

3. After the interview

If I didn't get the job, I asked for feedback. Why the employer didn't feel that I was the best candidate. I also didn't let this part of the process dent my confidence. It will happen to most people at some point in their lives. I came to understand that a rejection can be given for any number of reasons. There might simply have been someone who had more experience than I did, or it was possibly a straight choice between myself and another candidate.

I quickly learned to accept the situation when I didn't get a job, and started looking again as soon as possible. Preferably the same day, because I was determined to succeed. I certainly didn't want to miss any new opportunities which were being advertised on the job boards. Also sending my CV to others helped me adjust to searching again. I always tried to think of it as being for the best, and that the right job was still waiting for me to find it.

4. Where was my career path taking me?

The simple answer was through a number of interviews, and jobs. But that was fine. I was still on the path for the role I ultimately wanted. I was interviewed early in my journey by the Head of HR at Entertainment UK, a division of Woolworths Plc. I felt an instant connection to the company when I walked into the reception area, but the interview was far from easy. When I was offered the job, I jumped up with excitement!

Lorraine told me afterwards that she had interviewed several experienced candidates with an HR background, but I was the one who stood out from the rest. My passion and drive to succeed had shone through what I said to her. It had quickly become apparent that I didn't regard the job as simply another HR role. During my time at Woolworths, I was to experience an entire employee lifecycle ending in redundancy, and the winding up of the company in 2009. This taught me that despite HR's humble roots, and good intentions, all of us have to be resilient. Our profession is anything but cosy chats and cups of tea, as some people seem to believe.

I am thankful now that I experienced this. It taught me to be commercially aware, and that I needed to fully understand how a business operated. Once the initial shock was over, I could see that the situation hadn't happened because of anything I had done. The change it created presented me with the opportunity to broaden my knowledge of HR, and progress my career. I did a lot of soul searching at the time. This carried me through what was an upsetting experience, and had a positive effect on my long term wellbeing. I was to be made redundant a second time by another organisation. I was more able to deal with my feelings then, because of the experience I had at Woolworths. Redundancy can have a negative association. Employees worry about how they will pay the bills, and find alternative employment. Self esteem can hit rock bottom. There can also be a feeling of no longer having a contribution to make. Thinking this through made me realise that whilst my role was redundant, it didn't mean that I was, I still had a long career ahead of me, with extensive experience to offer a prospective employer. I couldn't, nor should I, give up!

When I was able to recognise this and change my mindset, I found the perfect role. I began to look at life positively again, and that's when the magic began to happen. I can honestly say that once I discovered this, I didn't look back. It would have been easy to give up, but I thought about what I had already achieved in my career, and where I still wanted to be. It was how I dealt with this gap in my employment history that made all the difference. It influenced the direction I took, and assured me that I did have something to offer my next employer. Nevertheless the United Kingdom was going through the worst recession seen in decades. The retail industry slumped, and this was where I had most of my experience. After leaving Woolworths in early 2009, all I could get was temporary work. Until 2011 when I was offered a permanent role by Circle Express, an air freight company at Heathrow Airport. I was able to step out of HR Administration into a more senior role, and I became an HR Consultant.

KEEP GOING!

The job of dreams is waiting for you, to find it.

PART II: LEARNING ALONG THE WAY

CHAPTER 4: Looking After Your Wellbeing

Without good physical and mental health a working life can be very difficult, if not impossible.. I hope that my thoughts, and experience, in looking after my own wellbeing will help you.

1. That "Monday morning" feeling

I soon discovered that the secret to having a successful week began with a daily routine, and being well organised. That how I started my day could make all the difference. Having a positive mindset, and being in control of the small things made me feel more confident. I was also surprisingly more productive.

It wasn't unusual for me to feel that the weekend had flown when Monday came around again. "The Mondays" happened when I had to leave a relaxing weekend behind, to enter the rigid structure and chaos of a working week. From that wonderful place of being able to choose when I ate; what I wanted to wear, and how I would spend my two days of freedom. I soon lost track of time at the weekend, and it's easy to see how it often felt that I was swinging from one extreme to another when I went back to work. The working week had a very different structure. Trying to stop what I was doing for a break, at a specific time. Dressing in a particular way, and when there were more things to do than time allowed. Whilst my diary always seemed to be filled with meetings, relating to those one hundred and one things on my to do list. Leaving me feeling inadequate and unprepared to start the week, which was much worse than a simple dislike of Mondays.

I discovered that by having a simple routine before I set out for work made me feel more in control of my life. I didn't allow worry or anxiety to intrude on any of my free time. Here are some of the things I did:

a. Getting my To Do List in order.

This was vital. It helped me put a stop to internal complaints that it was almost Monday again, and which served to increase my sense of dread. I wrote everything down I needed to do in the coming week. Sometimes the list was smaller than I had persuaded myself it would be, so much easier to achieve than I thought. You can even find an App for this now, if you want to try it.

b. Preparing my clothes for the week

This was an enormous help. I used to waste a ridiculous amount of time every morning, in trying to decide what to wear. It was stressful, and caused me to rush when I didn't need to. I felt so much better knowing that I had planned my outfits. I laundered the clothes and ironed them in advance, so that they were ready and waiting in my wardrobe.

c. Creating a food plan

I seemed to be even worse at deciding what to eat, and I wanted to stop buying the expensive and bland sandwiches I ate. I knew that I would have to plan my meals in advance, if this was going to happen. An organised, weekly, food shop would be essential and thinking about what would be suitable to eat at work. Cutting up fruit, and vegetables, to have as snacks was important too. I soon learned that having a healthy diet helped me feel good, and had an impact on my motivation.

I used a simple spreadsheet, to itemise the meals I was going to have. I thought this would take a long time to do, but it was only ten minutes once I was used to it. I found too that I was saving money, as I had a shopping list and could focus on what I needed to buy.

d. Having an event or activity to look forward to

Perhaps meeting a friend after work for dinner; catching up on a TV series, or having a cosy night in to read a book? The week was about so much more than work, and I tried to have a treat whenever I could.

e. Social media

Weekends and evenings were a great time to prepare and schedule my tweets for Twitter. I also used to prepare my Linkedin campaigns, and blog posts in advance. Tools like Hootsuite became my best friends.

f. Getting my gym bag ready

If my bag and outfits were packed, I was less likely to put off going to the gym until the following day or run the risk of not going at all. Leaving me feeling disappointed, and definitely unhealthy.

g. Time to relax

This sometimes felt like a mountain to climb and still does, but it's important. The last thing I wanted to do was feel stressed at the start of the week. So trying to relax as I was getting ready for work made a lot of difference.

I learned that even if I could only manage to do some of the things on my list, this would go a long way towards setting me up for a much easier and organised week.

2. Just be yourself

It can be difficult at times not to be nervous or anxious at work when starting a new job, or in a challenging situation. Trying to copy someone else's behaviour will not make you seem more credible, or authentic. More often than not it will result in you appearing to be more nervous than you are about getting the job done properly, and will highlight a lack of experience to the people you are trying to impress.

I have learned that we come across as being much nicer when we are ourselves. It's easier to form genuine relationships; build trust, and work as a team. Authenticity and credibility are vital to an HR career, and your personal development. They make Human Resources exactly that, an essential part of being human. As soon as you start to be yourself at work, this can significantly increase your credibility. Once your colleagues get to know the real you this makes you approachable, and can open the door to a wealth of opportunity which will grow and enhance your career. I have seen it happen many times. Not only HR, and at all levels.

Conversely many people prefer to behave in a corporate and professional manner at all times, without letting their guard down. To preserve a certain image. Perhaps the fear of vulnerability is at the root of it, and how their colleagues will perceive them? Making them reluctant to reveal their true selves. I completely understand the need for this in a new role, when an employee might still be assessing the boundaries. It's the sensible option, but I still think it is equally important that elements of our personalities are reflected in our work. So that others can relate to us. Whether it's in a spreadsheet, presentation, or training session doesn't matter. It simply needs to happen.

3. Your mental health

Maintaining our authenticity and credibility extends to the work life balance. Personal space, relationships, and mental health wellbeing. I will talk more about taking care of mental health in the next chapter, and the employees and managers in the businesses and companies where we work. Suffice to say here that whilst it is important to promote the wellbeing of others, we cannot adequately support other people without making our own mental health a priority. It is something all of us can promote, and actively participate in.

How we are feeling can vary in our daily life. It often depends on external circumstances, or is affected by significant events. Such as a birthday, or bereavement. Most of us will experience a traumatic event at some point. Not necessarily an isolated incident, but something which will stay with us. When we have good mental health, we are able to cope with the stresses of everyday life. Adapt to the environment we are in, and situations. Also, engage with them. If we don't have this, it is easy to feel detached from people and the environment. To lack confidence in our ability to cope. Most of all, we are unable to freely express our emotions, and maintain healthy relationships.

With this in mind, it's easier to see the importance of caring for our own mental well being. Here are some quick and easy tips, that I have found helpful in the past:

a. Talking about my feelings

Especially if I was going through a difficult time. An open conversation with friends, and family, halved the problem. They could often offer help, and guidance. If not, then simply having had a conversation with them made me feel a lot better.

b. Learning to accept myself

This was an important part of having good mental health. Not comparing myself to others, as this could damage my self-esteem. Even though it might be difficult to do, with the influence of social media and the unrealistic perception that all of us had to be perfect. Instead, always trying to be myself, acknowledging any positive qualities and attributes I had.

c. Exercise

When I went running three times a week, I felt on top of the world. Although I tried I didn't become a gym bunny, but getting out in the fresh air could change my perspective on life. It definitely had a positive impact on my mental health, I found that I worried less; slept better, and it was fun to do.

d. Diet

A well-balanced diet complimented my exercise routine. It helped make me feel healthier, and happier.

e. Relaxation

As with everything now, you can find an app for it! You don't need to try expensive yoga classes or massages. Although these are great too. Relaxation techniques helped me switch off and relax, when it was difficult to stop thinking about work.

4. Don't forget your Goals

a. Keep a Note of Them

This was important in helping me keep on track, and stay focused. To continue taking action, to achieve whatever I had set out to do. So grab a diary, planner, or even a whiteboard if you are like me. Write them down, as this can help increase your motivation, but be realistic about what you can physically do. Break the actions into smaller pieces which you can work through one step at a time. Most of all, be patient, Rome wasn't built in a day! It's also highly unlikely that you'll get the wage rise you asked for, if your employer's business is going through a difficult time. Plans can be changed, and you may be better advised in that situation to find another job.

b. Believe in Yourself

Believing that you can do it is one of the most important parts of successfully achieving a goal, and you may surprise yourself.

c. Go for it!

Post it notes are fantastic. I made them my new best friend, by writing the smaller parts of my goals on them. Using one for each day, and putting them in a place where I could see them. Mine sat comfortably on a mug next to my kettle, as it was the first place I went to in the morning. You are right. I am still a tea junkie! And this may remind you too, as it did me, of the next step that I needed to achieve in my journey through HR.

5. How to stay motivated when Distance Learning

At the start of 2018 I began distance learning with ICS Learn. When I told my colleagues and friends about it, some of them said that they wouldn't have the discipline to do the work. Undertaking a distance learning course is a responsibility, but I was determined to achieve my career goals. This made further study essential. Distance learning was convenient, and adaptable to my lifestyle. I learned so much from it, except how to stay motivated. I had to develop this quality myself to stay focused.

I adopted a positive approach to my CIPD Level 7 studies, by ensuring that I had everything I needed to hand. I found that there was nothing worse than getting into an assignment and having to stop because I had forgotten something. These are my top tips for distance learning:

a. Be organised

Make sure that you have all of your equipment to hand, I had my iPad for my virtual bookshelf, and used my laptop to keep track of how far I needed to read for each assignment. This stopped me from getting ahead of myself whilst still being able to capture the information I needed.

b. Take regular breaks

A five minute break every hour gave my eyes a rest, and was an opportunity to give my body a well earned stretch. It helped to keep my mind fresh, and stopped me from feeling overwhelmed. I often used this time to reflect upon what I had learned. How I could use it in my working life.

c. Map your progress

I had a large wall calendar above my desk which helped me keep on top of things, and see how far I had come. It also helped me keep my end goal in sight, and understand how flexible I could be on those weeks when I had other commitments.

d. Get a different perspective

I used my network a lot when it came to my studies, and I attended HR Hour every week on Twitter. I discovered a lot of different points of view which in turn helped me understand the arguments for, and against, certain processes. When I needed further information on a particular subject I read HR blogs, and asked questions on the Linkedin CIPD forum. This gave me the inspiration to carry on, and helped support my learning journey.

e. Reward yourself

When an assignment was graded, I took the time to reward myself for a job well done. It wasn't always easy to remain motivated, so a little treat went a long way in encouraging me to take the next step on my learning journey.

f. Take time out

Just because I was studying didn't mean that I couldn't have any time for fun! I saw friends and family which helped clear my mind, and relieve the stress I might otherwise have felt. I spent one of my days off with them, walking around Burghley House. It was great to be in the fresh air, and catch up.

Finally, whatever stage you have reached in your studies or job search, the best advice I can give is to try and stay focused. Well organised too. Always keeping the end goal in sight. It is vital to keep going. However difficult that might sometimes seem. Looking after yourself and your health along the way. ...The journey through HR can be a wonderful one. I promise.

Never forget that you can do this. Be passionate, & strong!

CHAPTER 5: Mental Health in the Workplace

We learn our HR skills not only from studying and taking exams, but while we are doing the job. Wisdom comes from this experience, and other areas of life. It's impossible to tell you everything in this book about being an HR professional, but I am going to touch on a few topics in this chapter and the next. Simply to give you an insight into some of the things you could be involved in, as part of an HR team. Just as I was when I started out in my career, and still am.

1. Is your Employer aware, and supportive?

Long gone are the days when employees could be expected to leave their problems outside the workplace. There is a greater emphasis now on organisations being proactive when it comes to supporting an employee's health, and wellbeing. Many have Employee Assistance Programmes, and Occupational Health facilities. Whilst some are taking this one step further, in also having mental health first aiders. Nevertheless a significant number of employees still continue to hide their problems from the employer. Usually because of the stigma which they anticipate will be attached to revealing them.

It is often said that employees are a company's greatest asset, but this doesn't mean that an employer will treat them well. A business is more often than not focused on its objectives, and results. Sometimes with little thought on how these will be achieved. Whilst happy and valued employees breathe life into a workplace. Without its people, a business can't exist. It's not rocket science to take this one step further! If those employees are enabled, and allowed to become high performers, an organisation will see a return on its investment in their wellbeing.

It is important that employers remain open minded. Looking out for signs that an employee might need extra support, even temporarily. It should be considered acceptable for them to talk about their feelings at work, and the life experiences they are going through. Good, and bad. All of us need to speak up! Otherwise the stigma attached to this will continue, without reaching a point where it is being dealt with more positively.

Mental Health is not a new topic and has become even more important because of the ever increasing pressure of daily life. Whether that is in the home, workplace, our relationships, or otherwise. Also the view taken by social media, that perfection is normal. It is likely that employees suffering from mental health issues will:

a. get into conflict with colleagues;
b. find it harder to juggle multiple tasks;
c. be unable to concentrate;
d. take longer than usual to complete a task,
e. be less patient with customers and clients.

2. The effect of Stress

Stress has become a major cause of long term absence from work for both manual and non-manual workers. Often involving lengthy absences, and even termination of contracts of employment. It is usually related to an excessive workload; frustration with poor management; lack of support, and unrealistic targets. Stress at work can also affect personal life, putting a strain on relationships outside the workplace. Studies conducted by Mind Charity have revealed startling findings, regarding the employee's behaviour:

a. calling in sick to avoid work when asked how workplace stress had affected them;
b. resigning, or considering this, when asked how

workplace stress had affected them;

c. feeling unable to talk openly with a line manager about feeling stressed;
d. wishing to do more to improve staff wellbeing, but not feeling that they had the right training or guidance to do so.

3. What happened to me

I don't believe that there is a one size fits all approach which can be adopted when dealing with mental health. I try to build strong working relationships with those around me. Hoping that if anyone does need someone to talk to I will be the person with whom they feel most comfortable, and can approach for support. I believe that it's important to do this. I have faced a lot of difficult HR situations, in dealing with employees across the years. These include gambling addiction; alcoholism, and post-natal depression. Also Post Traumatic Stress Disorder or PTSD; mental health problems caused by financial difficulties, and severe depression. Whilst these circumstances couldn't be foreseen, if there had been adequate support mechanisms available in the first instance then the employees' circumstances could have been handled differently.

These weren't, "just people at work." I took their difficulties home with me. This had a huge impact on my emotional wellbeing. At times I didn't sleep, or eat very much. I didn't feel comfortable talking to my family and friends about what was happening to me, but all this has changed. I now have a very close and supportive network. It didn't suddenly appear. I had to take the first step, and having the conversations I needed was difficult. I didn't talk about individual cases, to breach their confidentiality and the employees' trust in me, but I was asking for help. Not for them, but myself! As soon as I did this, I felt so much better. Sharing what I was going through was in itself a form of therapy. I realised afterwards that it is important for all of us to have someone like this to talk to. Internalising emotions can damage our own wellbeing, and sometimes with lasting effects.

Having similar conversations in the workplace is important, but it can be difficult for an employer to instigate them. Especially if leaving personal life outside work has previously been considered the best approach. I have often seen that an employee's authenticity is encouraged when things are going well. Why should it be any different when he or she requires emotional support?
When I was researching this topic, I was surprised to find so much information available online for anyone to read. Not only employers. The prominent themes seemed to be taking care of yourself; taking care of others, and that two heads are much better than one. Taking a step back from this, isn't it simply a common sense approach? I am not saying that we should go from one extreme to the other, with employers' writing extensive policies. Questioning their employees every time they appear under the weather, or miserable. Having the right support mechanisms instead, if they should be needed. Simple things like training line managers on how to start a conversation with an employee about how he or she is feeling, and the reasons for this.

4. How Human Resources can help

    a. Promote an Employee Assistance Programme. These are not particularly expensive, and provide an impartial and specialist resource that all employees can use anonymously. Whilst you will not be told how it is used, you should still be able to obtain a report which indicates the type of calls being made. This will allow you to take a more proactive approach.
    b. Research the internet for management support guides, and put them on your company intranet. These are currently available free of charge on

the Mind Charity website.

c. Host a webinar on the subject of mental health. You can either do this yourself or sign up for one via Mind, ACAS or CIPD. Depending on who is hosting one when you look. Invite your managers to join you for the webinar, to reinforce a common purpose.
d. Be proactive in giving return to work interviews. If employees have been absent due to personal issues; stress, or depression. Ask them if there is anything you can do to help, or support them. As an HR professional if you are unsure what to do next, you can ask for guidance from your Occupational Health provider.

The following are some of the simple steps an HR professional can take, to enhance awareness of mental health in the workplace:

For more information on how to implement a mental health awareness campaign in the workplace, please visit the Mind Charity website, ACAS, or CIPD.

5. When a Business Ceases to Trade

On 15th January, 2018 an announcement was made that one of the United Kingdom's largest construction companies, Carillion, had entered into compulsory liquidation due to the banks' refusal to provide any further financial support. It resulted in a lot of questions being asked about the financial management of the business. Also nineteen thousand five hundred employees facing the harsh reality that their jobs would probably no longer exist. What should they do? Go to work as normal, or stay at home? This was only one of the many questions they had.

Having been a part of the collapse of Woolworths in 2008, I

knew that the Carillion employees would be feeling shocked and upset, irrespective of their length of service. A lot of people become passionate about the business they work for. Carillion was a large employer, and company that it would be difficult not to be proud of. In any insolvency procedure it is important to consider the employees' rights. Would they have a valid claim against the company for wrongful dismissal, and the recovery of unpaid wages? Even if they did, the amount awarded to them would rank in the liquidation as an unsecured debt. Any priority debts being paid before theirs, as happened in the earlier Woolworths case. Would the employees also be entitled to receive payment in lieu of notice, redundancy or holiday pay?

Unlike Woolworths which had entered into administration and continued to trade for a short time after the announcement, Carillion's fate seemed sudden and final. Employees had been notified of the likelihood of closure during the preceding weekend. This must have taken a heavy toll on their mental health, and wellbeing. When a business ceases to trade HR can play a supporting role in the situation. Helping employees complete any forms which are required, and focusing on the possibility of alternative employment. Ensuring that employment agencies have been contacted. Creating an email of frequently asked questions, and offering support to those who are unable to create a CV. Especially if they have been with the company for many years.

When the announcement was made in late 2008 that the Woolworths group was entering into administration, it was a moment in my early career that I will never forget. I quickly learned that being in business can be unbelievably harsh. If I was to survive in HR I had to toughen up, to be able to support the needs of other employees. That was my job! I also had to learn to deal with the many different reactions I was facing. Some employees didn't seem surprised about the decision, whilst others were shocked. Relief was evident too, and there were those who wanted to do everything they could to save the company. The majority were however distressed, and concerned for the future. When you work for an organisation like Woolworths which has a substantial heritage, there is often a loyal workforce and community feel to it. HR had to provide as much support to the employees as possible, and handle the situation with great sensitivity. Whilst treating each employee as an individual, and listening to his or her concerns.

HR was however rendered almost helpless once the official administrators arrived on site, but it was still a busy time for us. Simple requests like holiday entitlement and resignations had to be run past the administrators first. Most of the company contracts and assets were frozen, including employee assistance programmes unless the full fees had been paid for upfront. HR had to take on the role of handling these specialist areas, to the best of our ability. Speaking to the employees remained vital. As an HR administrator I went to pick and pack in the warehouse, helping get the orders out in time for Christmas. I was surprised to find a jovial atmosphere when I was there, because it looked as if Woolworths might at that point survive. It was great to see the stock moving again, after an incredibly slow two weeks, and I was thrilled to be a part of this.

Sadly on 12th December, 2008 we were told that the doors of this iconic company were closing, with final trading taking place on 6th January, 2009. From 12th December the HR team found five thousand employees queuing for advice on their redundancy pay; shares, and pensions. I remember going home that evening feeling completely numb, and being able to accurately visualise the contents of a redundancy form. We received so much gratitude as a team. Often tearfully given, and it made us appreciate the opportunity we had to work with some wonderful people. Also that by actively listening, and being supportive, this had an impact on those employees.

I contacted as many recruitment agencies as possible. Trying to find suitable employment for as many employees as I could. We held CV workshops, with interview skills' training. Some employees had been with the company for more than forty years, and this was their primary area of concern. We also invited recruitment agencies to visit us, and register candidates. This couldn't be done until all the information had been received from the administrators about the future of the business. As my former colleagues and I often said, there would be life after Woolworths. It was just hard to imagine life, without it.

SMALL CHANGES CAN HAVE A BIG IMPACT. SUPPORT MENTAL HEALTH AWARENESS IN YOUR WORKPLACE!

CHAPTER 6: A Supporting Role for Human Resources

1. Helping Employees cope with bereavement

I decided to include this topic because it can be very difficult to deal with as a member of HR. When I started work I didn't have any personal experience of bereavement on which I could draw. I knew little of the intense pain and grief which the loss of a loved one can cause, or the range of emotions that so often turn employees' lives upside down. Having a detrimental effect on mental health, and work performance. It seems strange that we don't talk about this, when it is something which will happen to all of us at some point. If we did we might feel more comfortable about supporting others when they are in this situation, and need our help.

An employer's duty of care to an employee doesn't cease, simply because grief is a sensitive subject. I understand completely that not everyone will want to talk about their loss. Whilst managers and employers might not be sure of the best approach. It may also be all well and good applying a company policy on bereavement leave, but when the situation arises is this policy fit for its purpose? Is it flexible enough? Does it provide adequate support and consideration, for the on-going effects of the employee's loss? Are Managers adequately equipped to deal with, and understand, this process?

Employers need to assess the situation carefully when an employee returns to work. He or she needs to be advised as quickly as possible of any support that can be given, to minimise anxiety and stress. A frequently asked question is whether close team members should be made aware of the situation. I have heard stories of colleagues unknowingly asking a bereaved employee if he had been on holiday. A situation like this could easily have been avoided in a conversation with the employee. Asking how they would like to deal with the matter, and following their wishes.

The long term effects of grief can escalate into mental health difficulties, and depression. So it is important to be guided by the employee, in relation to how much support they actually need. Understandably it is a difficult balance to get right. The HR team will try to support an employee in every way possible, but they also don't want to make him or her feel overwhelmed by their concern. Simply letting the employee know that you are there for them, and maintaining a good level of communication, allows for support without its becoming an intrusion.

2. Simple ways to boost Employee productivity

Productivity has been a talking point in HR for a long time. Whether it is the intention to boost it or identify the cause of poor performance, being considered productive in today's working environment is harder now than it has ever been. The conflicting information on how many hours per week we should work is set against presenteeism. Also the importance of achieving a desirable work life balance. It's easy to see how productivity can be lost in translation.
I have found that the following can help organisations support their employees positively, whilst increasing productivity levels:

a. By offering remote, or flexible working. Is there really any need for an employee to be continually in the workplace? Why shouldn't employees start work, and finish earlier? If they are early birds and are at their most productive in the morning, employers would be crazy not to take advantage of this. In the case of an international business, flexibility could provide greater coverage for departments. If an organisation needs part time employees and is struggling to find them, why don't they consider parents who often can't take on these opportunities because of the inflexible hours? It makes sense to tap into a market which is often overlooked, and may well be hiding talented workers. If an employer is prepared to make positive changes by introducing this flexibility, it could provide a boost to productivity.

b. Show your employees that you value them. This is a basic point, but to employees it may mean a lot more than an employer realises. A simple acknowledgment of a job well done can make a world of difference to workplace relationships, and be another enabler of productivity. There are several ways that companies can do this. Offering training opportunities; creating a continuous feedback culture; recognition schemes, or by simply saying thank you. The return on investment of using this simple step might surprise you. It could even be the key to reducing staff turnover, and retaining existing talent.
c. Ask your employees' opinions. Speaking of an open and honest culture, this is an easy way of finding out the information you need to know. If you host an engagement survey every year that's a great idea, but it's also essential to process the data which has been collected. Is the employer doing it in a meaningful way, or is it being used as a tick box exercise? The results provide an opportunity to make changes for the better.
d. Actively support employee wellbeing, as we have already considered in chapter 5, and there

is still more to be done. Not all employers actively promote good mental health in the workplace. Some do offer gym membership packages; access to private healthcare, and fresh fruit Tuesdays! Supporting health and wellbeing is a complex area. We don't have the same needs so the main thing is to stress the importance of self care, as a means of supporting mental health wellbeing.

e. One size doesn't fit all. We are now working with a possible maximum of five generations in the workplace. What one person needs at a certain stage in his or her life, another won't find useful. It's important that we look for ways which will appeal to everyone. An employee returning from maternity leave will have different needs to another who is looking to retire.

3. Are annual appraisals still relevant?

I believe that HR, and management, have relied for too long on annual appraisals. A tool that was designed by our predecessors, but is likened now to household chores! Something which is unfulfilling; stressful, and more than likely not fit for its purpose. I got rid of them completely in a previous role. I thought they were rigid; impersonal, and artificial. I used check in meetings instead, to create an open and ongoing dialogue with my team. There was absolutely no point in waiting twelve months for one of them to tell me that they would like some support. The moment would have long gone, and demotivation set in.

Whilst from an employee's point of view, the appraisal is often associated with criticism and negative feedback. This is almost always linked to repercussions which can make it feel like a disciplinary matter, instead of what it is intended

to be. A constructive meeting that provides an opportunity for learning from mistakes. Most people do however link negative feedback with unpleasant consequences. When it should instead be a matter of celebrating those mistakes, as opportunities to learn. Employees may not need an annual appraisal, but they do need guidance and support. This has to come from their line manager who must be willing to give it. This behaviour can't be taught, but must again follow the example set by more senior management.
Getting managers to accept new ways of working can be a hurdle in itself. It is crucial to ensure that they are comfortable in providing, and receiving, feedback. Employees generally want to know how they are performing in their roles. Although some will be more open to this than others, and it is essential that they are given the correct training to encourage effective communication. Also advising employees that training is required as a way of helping, and supporting them. Not as a criticism of their lack of skills, or knowledge.

The conversations we may have instead of an annual appraisal don't have to be complicated, or the result of overthinking the situation. Asking employees how they feel about their job, and the challenges they currently face, can generate a lot of useful information for a manager. It can enable better quantification of workloads. Seeing where more efficient ways of doing things can be introduced, and encourage continuous improvement. This approach helps gain trust within the organisation between the employee and employer, by enabling an effective two way conversation. A real opportunity to work as a team when that's all we really want. I prefer to replace annual appraisals with positive performance strategies. Enabling an open and regular means of communication, so that performance is measured in real time without any surprises.

4. What about curriculum vitae?

A CV doesn't usually give enough detail about a candidate's potential. Only what he or she has done before. It cannot tell us if a young person will be the next Star of the future, because it doesn't provide an opportunity to show this. So we use other processes to learn more about the candidate. Application forms; video or telephone interviews; selection days, and panel interviews. When we offer the job, we may even get a screening company to check the validity of the entire CV.

It can be easy to assume from this that no longer using CVs wouldn't be too disruptive. Online applications are generally quick, and easy to use. This can make them seem as if they are streamlining the recruitment process, which is in reality a smokescreen. Although they have made submitting the application easier, the process still encounters the same problem as in the past when only a CV was used. It allows a large number of people to believe that all of them have an equal chance of being considered for the role. When the number of applications for most jobs has become so unmanageable, that recruiters have to look for ways of reducing their number. As a rule this doesn't include reading every single one! This means that the ideal candidate for the job can be overlooked.

How much easier it would be if we didn't use CVs in the recruitment process, and looked instead for a unique approach to recruitment. Yes it can be scary to use a blank page when dealing with people management, but isn't that what true innovators do? They find a better way. I believe that we shouldn't stop looking for a more effective recruitment process, or trying to create improvements in the workplace. The more efficient the processes become the better it is for everyone, and the HR profession.

HR SUPPORT FOR MANAGERS AND EMPLOYEES HAS AN

IMPORTANT IMPACT!

CHAPTER 7: Networking & Mentorship

Life isn't only about what we receive, but what we can also give back to others. My journey through HR hasn't only been about me, and the help I received from colleagues who were more experienced than I was. It has been rewarding to be able to give back what I could, to other colleagues and those who were joining the profession.

I owe a large part of my success to the networking I have done across the years, and acting as a Mentor.

1. The Power of Networking

You have probably heard the expression that it's not what you know, but who you know. Many of the exciting developments in my career have come about as a result of networking. It expanded my knowledge; opened doors, and even presented me with job opportunities. All from simply getting myself known.

During 2015, I went along to Northants Business Club for an evening of business networking. The club consisted of professionals from various industries, and backgrounds. This gave me the opportunity to learn, and meet other like minded people. Some were business owners. Others like myself were from larger companies, so it was a good mix. I met people I had only previously "talked to" online, and it was amazing to meet HR professionals who ran their own businesses. I was also looking to join the Northamptonshire CIPD committee later that year which would involve helping out at branch run events; discussing future trends, and keeping up to date with the latest from the world of HR.

Helping in my local branch raised my professional profile, as well as enhancing my Continuous Professional Development (CPD). I was able to learn more about the CIPD; employment law, and the future of HR. Networking can however be a daunting prospect especially at first, but I found that once I had attended my first couple of events I started to enjoy myself. It's important to bear in mind that if we are not out there raising our profile, no one else will be doing it for us! Here are my seven top tips, if you are new to networking:

a. Take your time. Find the right networking group for you. Research the content, and discussion points. Many networking groups have their previous minutes, or meeting details, available on their websites. So you can see if the topics are of interest.
b. Get tweeting! Social media is a helpful way of looking at discussion points from like minded professionals. At the time of writing this book, you'll find me mostly on Twitter. Many groups and companies now have a Twitter page giving short updates on current HR trends.
c. If you are doing face to face networking, everyone loves a freebie! So bring yours to the meeting. I took some of my Employers' branded pens with me to the Northants Business Club, and they went down a storm. Don't forget your business cards or contact details. A lot of people will also find you on Linkedin after the event, so make sure that your profile is up to date before you attend.
d. Get to know people. Introduce yourself, and more importantly be yourself. People are not always sold on a product or service, but enjoy doing business with those they know and trust. So take your time when getting to know others. Keep in touch after the meeting, to get the most from your relationships, and you never know

when your knowledge will be useful to someone else.

e. Take notes. When you ask for a business card after having a great conversation with someone, make brief notes on the back of it. This will help you to be more specific in any follow up conversation.
f. Focus on making a small group of solid connections. Meet a few people, and create a memorable dialogue to establish lasting relationships.
g. Join in. Don't be afraid. Wait for a natural break in the group conversation, to introduce yourself. Other people also enjoy meeting someone new.

2. The CIPD Steps Ahead Programme

If you have already been for your first HR interview, how did it make you feel? Maybe you can look back and smile about being nervous, as I do! Not knowing a lot about HR at the time made me feel this way, whilst wanting the job more than anything else in the world. I realise now that it doesn't have to be like this, if approached in a different way. Having a mentor can be the answer.

I joined the CIPD Steps Ahead Mentoring Programme, during 2012. This was aimed at young adults, aged between eighteen to twenty four years, who had been referred to us by Jobcentre Plus. Mentors were appointed to talk about chosen careers. We helped with CVs; interview techniques, and to build the mentee's confidence so that he or she would be ready for the workplace. I dedicated around one hour per week to each mentee I had.

The responses and feedback I have received since then, from people I successfully helped into employment, has been staggering. It was wonderful to see how motivated they became in the sessions we had, and looked forward to building a solid foundation for their careers. One of my successful mentees was a recent graduate. Although he was incredibly intelligent, he lacked the confidence to go for the role he wanted. We worked together over a period of six weeks, as recommended by the programme. We started by identifying his chosen career path before building on an existing CV, to target specific industries. Even this initial step proved to be a significant boost to his confidence.

The mentees explained to me that there weren't adequate mechanisms in place to support their transition into the world of work. A professional career advisor was someone they would have liked to see regularly before they were due to leave college or school, or graduate from University. This would have enabled them to understand how to correctly structure a CV, prepare for the workplace, and gain help with interview techniques. Going a long way towards boosting their confidence! Whilst this remains the case, it surely has to be a factor in persuading more professional people to get involved with programmes like Steps Ahead, which incidentally is still running. It's essential that we support the talent of the future. Otherwise we run the risk of more skill shortages in years to come.

3. Progressing to CIPD local branch mentoring

As part of the Northamptonshire CIPD branch in 2017, I was responsible for coordinating the peer mentoring scheme which had recently been launched. Helping our colleagues, and effectively supporting their careers in an ever changing environment, is again essential to the growth of the HR profession. Especially in view of the increasingly complex challenges that exist in today's workplace. By engaging with each other HR has the ability to truly innovate, and influence the future direction of the profession. Each one of us has something to offer irrespective of our workplace background;

qualifications, or job title. Someone will benefit from your experience.

So why not consider mentoring a fellow HR professional or someone new to the profession, as I have done? Now, or in the future. You never know. You might be helping to support a future HR Director, or Chief Executive.

4. What I learned from being a Mentor

Whilst being a mentor in the Steps Ahead programme, I discovered that HR has a lot to offer job seekers. Here are the main benefits we can share with others:

a. Experience. We get to know exactly what employers are looking for when it comes to recruiting. So for the new job candidate sometimes all it takes is an amended or updated CV; interview advice, and a little encouragement.
b. Connections. HR professionals network. We usually have access to hundreds of contacts via Linkedin; recruitment agencies; CIPD branch events; networking groups, and in our own workplaces. By utilising these contacts we can give opportunities to our mentees. It really is as simple as that.
c. Knowledge. We have expert insight into industry trends, and commercial knowledge that will assist job seekers. To ensure that they are clear about the companies they would like to approach as a prospective employer. This also reduces the risk of a mentee just applying for "any old job," or the wrong one for them.
d. Professionalism. We know how to present ourselves at interviews, and our experience so that it becomes something a prospective

employer can work with. School and university life is very different to the working world, and applying for a job can be a culture shock.

Mentoring is often thought to be time consuming. A long drawn out process which can sometimes deter people. In reality it can take as little as a couple of hours each month, and sometimes it's only to work on a CV. It feels great to help someone, and I also learned a lot along the way. Not only about people but the differences in the generations. How I could expand on my existing skills; recruitment challenges being faced by others, and of course the different industries. This exposure has helped me grow, as an HR Professional. Whilst as a mentor I have been ready to help in any way that I could. To listen; offer practical advice, and constructive criticism. If this is done in the right way, it can be a positive step. The mentee can often offer a different perspective or insight into their career; industry and aspirations. Believe it or not, mentees can help their mentors as much as we help them.

Branch mentoring was different to the Steps Ahead programme. Peer mentoring can strengthen our network; enhance leadership capabilities, and most of all support our colleagues. As a branch we have grown and progressed together, with a view to one day leading together. I believe that mentoring is the way forward for the HR profession, as a means of inspiring our future professionals and us.

BE AN
HR MENTOR,
AND
SUPPORT
YOUR
PROFESSION!

PART III: IT'S GREAT TO HAVE A BLOG

CHAPTER 8: What I Learned From My Blog

1. Creating a personal brand

Getting a branding right can be vital to your success. It is about how you present yourself to the world. The information you offer to other professionals, and understanding how they will see you. Getting it right can make a difference to a job application, or your career. It may represent you in a professional capacity before an interview, and help ensure that you are taken more seriously. If you have a blog which is part of your branding, followers will be able to identify your resources. Your experience; strengths, and skills. Blog posts showcase what you have to offer a prospective employer. It's also advisable to take part in active discussions on social media platforms, like Linkedin and Twitter.

By being active in these online forums, you will be engaging and interacting with other HR professionals. It's a great way to consider different viewpoints. Find ideas for the projects you are working on, or learn to understand and overcome difficult challenges in the workplace. My blog posts and Tweets have opened so many doors during my career, I have met some incredible people whom I now speak to regularly. I have enhanced my network which has given me support. I have also been able to help them. I now have a sponsorship deal with ICS Learn, and I am very grateful that they have made so much of this possible.

2. My top blogging tips

When I started blogging on November 8th, 2015 I didn't think that people would read my posts. Let alone see the doors it would open for me once it was up and running. Although it can be time consuming and demanding, blogging and social media have helped transform my career. I want to share the following with you, and hope these tips will be helpful:

a. Your career path is as unique as mine has been. Don't let a lack of confidence deter you from making a start. If you are waiting until everything is perfect, your blog might not happen. You will always find other HR blogs to compare to your own. You may well inspire someone to pursue their goals if you start blogging now. Or look for a job they imagined was beyond their capabilities.
b. Make the blog your own. There's no point getting out there, if you intend to copy someone else's work. You may feel foolish doing your first few posts because you believe that you have nothing to offer, but everyone has something to give. Make your posts as authentic as possible. Embrace your qualities, and opinions. Don't try to be like someone else. You don't need to be.
c. A word of caution, if you are sharing experiences in a post. As an HR professional you will be dealing with confidential matters. Most people wouldn't believe what we see or hear at work, but please don't be tempted to name specific cases. Use case studies instead, to convey what you'd like to talk about.
d. Post regularly, and often. Planning ahead as much as possible, to cover holidays and times when you know you will be busy doing other things. Followers will start to look out for your posts. Don't post something simply because it's due, if you don't really have anything to say. A lot of people may read what you have written, and an ill considered post can cost you followers. Possibly even the opportunity of a job you are

applying for.

e. Most of all, don't forget to have fun with your posts. Followers will be able to tell whether you have enjoyed writing them, and it's always better to be in a happy place.

3. In the Blog Squad again

I was ready to get back to my studies in Autumn, 2018. I had experienced a lot of major change in my personal life. Buying a house; having my step children for the summer, and welcoming a French Bulldog into the Ellis household. Bron is absolutely adorable. Much to my delight, I also discovered that I was to be in the blog squad again at the CIPD Annual Conference and Exhibition. The first event I took part in during 2016 was an absolute blast, and I couldn't wait to do it again. The fabulous bloggers I met had carried on "talking" to me in conversations on Twitter.

This was going to be the 71st Annual Conference on Leading the People Profession. It would continue the previous years' focus on the world of work, and its future. The pace of change had become greater. There was an expectation that people focused professionals would need to constantly adapt and change, to meet the needs of those around them. Apart from free training events, including one for LGBT on how to make the workforce more inclusive, there would be some amazing speakers and presentations. Events discussing race at work, and flexible working. All of which I wanted to take part in, and listen to.

4. The Blog Awards, 2019

If that wasn't enough, I was thrilled and honoured to be nominated for the 2019 UK Blog Awards. I was given first place, and I couldn't have done it without all the support I received from my followers. So if any of you are reading this, a huge thank you!

My blog is not only an integral part of my HR journey, but it is also very important to me in another way. I created HR Acts of Kindness because of it, and which I will tell you more about in the next chapter. I had stepped outside my comfort zone again; found the confidence to take the first step in posting, and reached out to others to widen my network and influence. I didn't give up when I had doubts about what I was doing. I definitely had a few of those at the beginning! Instead I continued posting, and I did what I said I was going to do. I carried on reaching for the Stars.

JOIN IN THE FUN, AND START A BLOG. REACH FOR THE STARS!

CHAPTER 9: HR Acts of Kindness

1. The first challenge

I wanted to start a chain of positive events in 2016 that would help members of HR motivate and support others, so I launched my first in a series of HR Acts of Kindness. I set challenges on my blog for five days; asked my colleagues to complete them, and tweet or email their stories to me based on the theme. I created the hashtag, #HRActofKindness It didn't cost any money, and was simply a way of brightening someone else's day. I also asked them to find five others who would join in with spreading the word, and continue the chain. These are the challenges I set for the first week:

a. If a colleague is having a bad day, find out what you can do to help and support them.
b. Get in touch with a former colleague, or connection on Linkedin. Have a coffee and chat, with someone you haven't seen recently.
c. When it comes to that Friday feeling it's important to celebrate the end of the week, and take a break. Not to be "talking shop" for once, with your colleagues.
d. It can be difficult to get back into routine on Mondays. So do something that will make your colleagues smile, and be glad to be in your team.
e. Create your own #HRActofKindness by listing five more challenges that can be completed across a working week.

Since the challenge began I have connected online with people from all over the world. Including New Zealand; South Africa, and the United States of America. This took me outside my comfort zone, and helped me grow as a professional.

2. The HR Star Challenge

I decided to follow the success of the first initiative with a new challenge, and #HRStar was born. The goal this time was for members of HR to invest in themselves, as a means of progressing their personal development. The key point was to establish what all of us wanted from our careers, and made us happy at work. The challenges I set were based on things I had done to advance my career, and which I have already talked about in earlier chapters so I won't repeat them. They included going outside our comfort zone; joining a local CIPD Committee; networking, and becoming a mentor.

3. Festive Acts of Kindness

I also created a festive #HRActsofKindness during November, 2016. The same rules applied, and the more people spreading kindness the better it was going to be. Here's the challenge list which is still relevant today, if you would like to make it part of your festivities:

a. Hold a mince pie and coffee morning in your workplace, or at a local nursing home for the elderly. Working together as a company to host an event like this can help a lot of people.
b. Boost morale within your team and the organisation you work for, by asking a school choir to sing carols in your workplace. This may sound bizarre, but I remember it happening in one of my jobs. It was great fun! We joined in; sang together, and drank hot chocolate. It was also an opportunity to give the school children an insight into our business, and offer work experience placements. There wasn't a single

person who left work that day without a smile on his or her face.

c. Utilise your resources. Promote your employee assistance programme, or support line. It may sound simple, but not everyone will realise it's there or that they can take advantage of the service it provides. Christmas can be a difficult time, and providing this service can mean a lot to some people.
d. Hold a shoebox appeal. You could do this for children living in foster care, or those who have fallen on hard times. The first time I ran this challenge my colleagues at Forterra put together donations for the homeless, at the Northampton Hope Centre.
e. Hold a charity cake sale and invite your colleagues; customers, and suppliers. This can bring people together, and raise money for the charity of your choice.
f. Help someone get ready to make an application for a new job in the New Year. This could be by updating their CV; interview technique, or adapting their job search so that they are targeting the right employer. All it can take is a few minutes, to help someone else land that dream job.
g. Collect donations for your local Children's Hospital, to buy toys for children who are going through a difficult time.
h. Arrange a Christmas themed lunch at work; book a table at a local restaurant, or order in a pizza. It's a great opportunity to get away from your desk, and spread the kindness, by spending a little time getting to know your colleagues.
i. Don't forget those who helped you get where you are now, when writing your Christmas

cards. I send cards to my tutors; former managers; colleagues, and those who have supported me in my career. Without them I wouldn't be here, and sending a card is a small act of gratitude.

j. There was a coffee bean sticker on the side of McDonalds' takeaway cups, in 2016. I collected the stickers, until I had enough for a free coffee token. I saved these to give to the homeless. Drinking coffee is good, but being kind and sharing it makes the experience even better. A lot of coffee shops take part in similar schemes, using printed cards.

4. Kindness is for Everyone

An #HRActofKindness challenge isn't only for HR. It can be adapted to suit any profession. Whilst kindness is a selfless act which is usually done without thought, or expectation. Here are a few of the other #HRActofKindness challenges I have set:

a. Send 3 positive messages to different people.
b. Be an encouragement to someone who needs support or help.
c. Ask new employees how they are getting on, and offer any assistance you can to help them settle in.
d. Be encouraging about someone's idea or project, and offer any guidance that might help them.
e. Compliment your Manager who may not get feedback very often.
f. Be kind to yourself, and give yourself some credit. Think about your own achievements. How far you have come. Sometimes we can be our harshest of critics.

5. It's about being there for each other

Another lesson I took from the Spice Girls when I set out on my HR journey was that a small team can accomplish much more, when the members support each other in their work and personal lives. Making time to help friends; family, and colleagues is one of our strengths which should be used consistently. When an HR department is fully in tune, a heavy workload becomes much lighter.

Success lies in working through our challenges together. Not only for the benefit of the HR profession, but for each of us individually. Difficult situations help keep us focused, and allow each one of us to develop our skills.

KINDNESS

is for every day, and everyone!

PART IV: LOVING WHAT I DO

CHAPTER 10: Success

1. An Independent HR Consultant

Wherever you are on your HR journey, it's important to carry on growing. I became an independent HR Consultant in 2020. I haven't stopped learning; keeping up to date with the legislation, and what is happening in the profession generally. My new role means that I have my own business, and I am still doing what I love. That's being part of HR. I work now with other companies and organisations, ensuring that they are correctly advised on best practice, to help them deal with difficult employment issues. Also, to grow their own businesses, by attracting the right employees. These are some of the tasks you will find me involved in:

a. Looking at internal HR practices, procedures, and guidelines.
b. Making sure company policies are implemented throughout the business.
c. Making recommendations as to how HR practices and operations can be improved.
d. Assisting with recruitment, and retention of employees.
e. Giving guidance on salary or other issues with remuneration.
f. Assisting with legal matters, including dismissals, disciplinary and grievance procedures.
g. Keeping clients up to date with legislation, and employment practice developments.

2. My Career of choice

Even though there have been a lot of difficult times, being an HR professional was throughout it all my career of choice.

When we work hard for something, the rewards are far greater than if it is simply offered to us. I enjoy the variety in HR work. As you have seen from this book, I never know what I'm going to find when I open the office door. Although this can be a challenge, it doesn't worry me because I now have a wealth of knowledge and experience on which I can draw. That didn't happen overnight, which makes it all the more valuable to have. Knowledge and experience give us confidence when we are faced with difficult situations. I also see being part of HR, as a means of helping others. When I speak with a client, I know that the advice and guidance that I give can support him or her in areas which might otherwise be intimidating.

I believe that we can, and should find our work enjoyable. It's beneficial to our overall well being. I hope that you will have found something in this book which inspires you, to follow your dreams as I have done. If you are in a job you dislike, the initial idea of "jumping ship" might be scary, but it's important to consider it. You could be stopping yourself from not only discovering the right career for you, but also hindering your personal development. Your dream career will not come to you! It happens because of hard work; commitment, and consistency. Also, through developing resilience. The challenges we face go a long way to shaping our careers, even if we don't realise it at the time. I made a scary decision years ago to change to HR, and I've not looked back.

3. Taking a long term view

Just as it's important not to stop learning, taking a long term view of your career is the best option. With this in mind and if you are still not sure of the path to take, here are five questions to ask which you may find useful:

a. What kind of HR professional do you see yourself as? Don't simply follow the trend. Find the path that is right for you. Do your research, to ensure that the job you want is right for you.

b. When applying for jobs, research the organisation you are going into. Look at their annual reports. Do a Google search to see how they are regarded as an employer. Find the answers to the questions that matter the most to you
c. Trust your gut instinct. Does the decision you are making feel right for you? I remember turning down an amazing job opportunity at a highly sought after organisation, because every part of me was saying don't do it. It turned out that I was right to make this decision, and I don't regret it.
d. Where do you see yourself in five years' time? Make sure you plan how you will manage your expectations to avoid disappointment. The path to a good career isn't always rosy, so make sure you are prepared for the occasional hiccup, and learn from it. Don't bring yourself down, with negative thoughts.
e. Review your performance regularly. Are you meeting your own expectations? Are you on track for where you want to be? Are there any development points that with a little work will help you along the way?

Your journey through HR will be what you make it, so don't settle for anything less than the best. Enjoy the plot twists, and remember to make the most of it all. Change isn't necessarily a bad thing. It can bring opportunities. Don't be tempted to put off pursuing your dream career because you believe the timing isn't right. When will be the right time, especially if you think of using the same reasons or excuses for another year? Think about what is important to you. What you really want to achieve. Nothing is more damaging to self

confidence than regret.
If you want to be successful in HR badly enough, then you can do it. Believe in yourself. You won't regret it!

4. Always making a difference

I have come to understand the impact we can have upon the businesses and organisations we represent. Looking back now, it was often a struggle to see how our profession could get beyond being regarded as a service department. There were so many hurdles to overcome. Who could influence HR's function; office politics; failure to recognise the value in good suggestions; leadership struggles, poor management skills, and more. There was also the overwhelming perception that, "anyone can do HR!" I have come across this opinion many times in my career. I could have been disheartened by it but I believe that it's up to us to continue demonstrating our professional contribution to the world of business, and which can sometimes mean challenging the status quo. There is a lot more to HR than simply winning hearts, and minds.

As an HR Professional we need to acquire the ability to influence at all levels. The challenges faced by the profession overall shouldn't be seen as a negative. Ultimately it's the variety that attracts most of us to the profession in the first place. After all when you work in a people profession, only one thing is guaranteed, and that is its unpredictability.

5. The future of Human Resources

A few years ago I walked into a boardroom, after some difficult changes had been made to the company structure. I was surrounded by a sea of confused, and weary faces. I knew long before the meeting that they were used to a strict command and control management style, so they weren't expecting the response they received from me. After introducing my team I simply asked them for their expectations, regarding HR. As you can imagine, a lot of people in the room were confused by the question, but once I had explained the true purpose of what we do it became the foundation of an effective working relationship. I believe that when we behave as if we are in an ivory tower and dictate how employees should work, it not only damages our relationships, but also impacts upon our ability to work efficiently. Giving a no win situation which isn't helpful to anyone.

HR is conditioned to stand up for what is right on behalf of both the employer, and employee. Consequently it needs to be objective. Resilient too, whilst challenging existing practices so that improvements continue to be made. It also encourages a collaborative, and inclusive culture. By working with the individuals in that boardroom, I was able to establish an effective communication between us. So that we could learn their concerns, and be able to ascertain what we could do to resolve them.

The future of HR is difficult to predict, as it is perpetually changing. External factors play a part in this. Currently the effects of Brexit; the Covid-19 virus; advances in technology, and mental health can all be listed as priorities. HR has a lot to deal with, and can't afford to drop the ball! Often in business the focus shifts to us, in the hope that we will be able to fix it magically. Whilst the truth of the matter is, we don't have all the answers. What we can do is mitigate the potential risks to a business, and drive performance through its people.

Getting our own house or team in order is a good place to start. Making sure that the basics are right by paying HR employees correctly. Recruiting the right people for the right roles in the first place, and being consistent about this, will significantly impact upon how the HR profession is perceived. Also to enable an effective partnership with businesses by enhancing our commercial awareness; knowing the industry; trends, and impacts. It needs to be underpinned by wholly understanding business operations. This will in turn encourage collaboration, and demonstrate where HR can truly add value. Building on trust and developing relationships is a powerful tool that shouldn't be underestimated. Taking time to understand others; their expectations; pain points, and development requirements has a positive impact.

I would also like to say that it isn't solely the responsibility of HR to facilitate change. It's more a case of how our profession is positioned to deal with it. Being open and managing expectations will support the changing business environment, and retain trust. I have found that it's important to understand exactly what Managers need, so that they are properly equipped to perform effectively. Empowering them in this way enhances their development. It allows them to work autonomously in making their own decisions, and encourages positive mental health.

Within the political and social uncertainty which we are currently facing, opportunity is also present. This includes being able to utilise existing resources; invest in the development of employees' skills to support the pressure of change, whilst playing to their strengths and talents. It's also a good idea to find out about their career aspirations. This will help in retaining valued employees at the same time as diversifying their skillset. HR will need to adopt new skills in order to be successful. Being flexible and adapting to the changing environment is essential. If we stand still as a professional body, we will fall behind. Instead of being in a position to deal with situations proactively, we will be continually firefighting. A frustrating outcome as the majority of HR Professionals prefer a proactive approach to their work, so finding the balance is vital.

A Final Thought...

My passion for HR continues to grow... I speak regularly at conferences and events, for both business and HR professionals. I am thrilled to be able to do this. That I am still following my dream. I have taken a positive approach throughout, and am able now to face challenges however difficult they might be.

This book came from the HR career I could only dream of... Once upon a time.

I wish you every success in the world.

NATALIE ELLIS
HR Professional

NEVER STOP FOLLOWING YOUR DREAMS!

I am an HR Consultant with 14 years of commercial HR experience and have worked for a number of high-profile companies including Woolworths Group, ASOS.com, Associated British Foods and Forterra PLC.

Having worked with such amazing companies in senior HR roles and as an HR Consultant, I have gained a lot of commercial experience which made me realise that some HR solutions are not accessible to smaller businesses which is a real shame because those companies have the potential for the biggest impact!

I am based in Daventry, Northamptonshire, however I travel regularly to London and beyond thanks to my ideal location. Additionally, I also work virtually with some of my clients which allows me to provide support to businesses throughout the UK (one of my clients is in Glasgow!).

In February 2020, I decided to set up Rebox HR with the aim of offering tailored HR support to small businesses from all industries. I am pleased to offer a personalised service, where we work together, and you receive dedicated and tailored HR support without a hefty price tag. Whilst the business may be new, it is already making a big impact; Rebox HR has been nominated for a Woman Who award and The Small Awards!

When you need HR support, it can be a stressful time, therefore you need a personalised service with your business in mind, not a cookie cutter solution. Additionally, if you only need support as a one off, you probably don't fancy signing your life away on forever contracts.

When people start looking for an HR service, they are often not sure what they need or what they're looking for so it helps to talk these thing over first, therefore if you're not sure what you need (you're not alone!) and would like to have a virtual cuppa and a chat, I offer a free 30 minute consultation to explore your options without the legal jargon, all with the best possible service in mind.

NATALIE ELLIS
HR Professional

www.reboxhr.co.uk
hello@reboxhr.co.uk

@ReboxHR
@rebox_hr

Have you ever thought about a career in HR and wonder what it would actually be like?

Are you already in a HR position but feel stuck, demotivated and cannot see where you can add value or make a difference?

Are you thinking that you're not the right "type" of person to get into HR?

If you have ever wondered those things, or are thinking about them right now, then stop (right now, thank you very much!)

I am Natalie Ellis and I was once that person thinking all of those things, comparing myself to my peers, never feeling that what I had to give would ever be enough. Now I am a regular HR keynote speaker, advising Managing Directors and CEO's on how HR can add value to their business strategies and the recipe for success is simple; roll up your sleeves and get involved.

LAUNCH YOUR HR CAREER IS TO HELP YOU:

- Get inspired
- Identify how to learn from difficult experiences
- Build your confidence
- Become more commercially aware
- How to keep going when the going gets tough

NO CAREER PATH IS EASY, IF IT WAS, IT WOULDN'T BE WORTH WORKING FOR, SO GRAB A CUPPA, HAVE A READ AND BE READY TO FOLLOW YOUR DREAMS, BECAUSE DREAMS DON'T WORK UNLESS YOU DO.

Cover Design: © Amy Bradley

Published by Rebox HR Ltd
ISBN 978-1-5272-7139-5

9 781527 271395